The Garden of Allah

By Emmet Fox

There is no god but God.
Thou shalt have no other gods before Me.

Wilderpubs@yahoo.com

ISBN 10: 1-61720-789-6
ISBN 13: 978-1-61720-789-1
First Edition

10 9 8 7 6 5 4 3 2 1

The Garden of Allah

Spiritual Key to Isaiah XXXV

Even those who love the Bible most are apt to make the mistake of looking upon it as merely a book, the greatest book ever written, no doubt, but still a book; whereas the truth about the Bible is that it is really a spiritual vortex in which spiritual power pours from the Absolute or Divine Plane into the physical plane or plane of manifestation.

But the Bible is not only the great source of spiritual truth, it is also the greatest collection of literary masterpieces that we possess. Almost every literary form is represented in the Bible, both in prose and poetry. History, biography, philosophy, the short story in its perfection — re-read some of the parables, for example — the epic, and even that supposedly modern form, the novel, are all found there. The Book of Job is really a play; and Revelation is a drama in form so strange and unprecedented that it remains in its entirety almost incomprehensible to most people, however much they may appreciate its separate details.

Above all, the Bible abounds in beautiful and powerful prayers and treatments, and this reason alone makes it for us the most important book in the world. This is because prayer is really the only thing that matters. The only way in which man can improve himself or his conditions, get a better knowledge of God — save his soul, in short — is by prayer. Prayer indeed is the only real action that makes things different.

Whenever you pray, you change your soul for the better. If the prayer is very short or the degree of realization very poor, the change it brings about may be small, but it occurs. It could not by any chance happen under any circumstances that any man or woman could pray for a single moment without some result for good following. Whenever you pray, your whole subsequent life is, as a consequence, somewhat different from what it would have been had you not prayed.

Now prayer is the only thing that does change the *quality* of the soul. Any other activity may make a *quantitative* change in the soul by adding experience, or by extending one's fund of knowledge; but it does not change the quality. Only prayer does that, and it is the quality of our soul that determines our destiny.

As long as there is no qualitative change in your soul, you will, under any given circumstances, say or do the thing that such a person as you are would say or do in such a case, because we never really act out of character. We are never other than ourselves. When we try to be other than ourselves by an effort of human will, we are just being ourselves all the more on that account. When you pray, however, you by that act become at least a slightly different man and, therefore, all your subsequent activities are different too. So prayer is the only thing that matters.

The word 'treatment' is a technical term that many of us use for prayer that is directed to the overcoming of a specific, practical difficulty, and the Bible is full of prayers and treatments of

every kind.

When you find yourself in any kind of trouble, no matter what it may be, whether you think it is caused by somebody else's conduct, or whether you feel that it is your own fault, or whether it seems to be no one's fault; in any case the only possible thing to do is to treat yourself about it. If you give yourself an efficient treatment — or it may be that several treatments will be necessary — then the difficulty, whatever it is, will presently disappear and you will find yourself out of your trouble. In other words, your prayer will be "answered," or, as we often say, you will make your demonstration.

But what is a treatment? Well, briefly, a treatment means that you recollect and realize the Truth about God until you have brought about a change in your own consciousness, whereupon, as a result of this change in yourself, the outer things completely change too. Note particularly that this does not mean merely that you gain courage or fortitude to meet your difficulties in a new spirit. That would be better than nothing, but not much better. The tremendous fact is that prayer does change things. As a result of the change in your mentality that results from your treatment, outer conditions change completely. Other people change their conduct and their attitude to you. Unpleasant things that would otherwise have happened do not happen, and good things that would not have happened had you not prayed, do happen and are brought about by prayer alone. *Prayer does change things.*

Now how is the necessary change in consciousness to be brought about? Or, in other words, how is a treatment made? Well the first thing to realize is that merely repeating a form of words is seldom any use at all. (That is better than nothing if you cannot do anything more. In fact, to cling to a single phrase may be the only thing that can save you in a great emergency; but fortunately such an extreme condition is very exceptional.) However, it is the change in feeling and conviction that matters. Any means that brings this about — and whatever means does it most quickly — is the best treatment. Whatever will raise your consciousness from the lower level of trouble to the higher level of freedom is a treatment. In many cases the quiet, thoughtful repetition of certain affirmations of Truth is sufficient, such as: "I am surrounded by the Love and Peace of God"; or "Divine Intelligence opens my way." Sometimes, and especially if you are faithful in daily prayer and meditation, the mere momentary "feeling out" for God will clear the most formidable difficulty with lightning-like rapidity; feeling out in thought, that is to say, without formulating any words at all. The reading of a page of any spiritual book that appeals to you or, above all, a few verses or a chapter from the Bible often constitutes a most powerful treatment. It is for this reason that the Bible has so many prayers and treatments included in its pages.

The literary arrangement in which we have received our Bible is very misleading in many instances. The division into chapters and verses was made comparatively recently. The original writers had nothing whatever to do with it, and it was done in an arbitrary fashion that paid very little attention to the subject matter concerned. So it happens that with a writer, such as Isaiah, for instance, his works have been run together with little or no regard to sequence of subject or chronological order, and then, so to speak, chopped up into approximately equal lengths which are called chapters. In addition to this, a great deal of material, splendid in itself but not belonging to the prophet called Isaiah, has been included. Of course this makes no practical difference at all, as long as we know about it. The actual writer of anything in the Bible does not matter in the least, because the true author of it all is the Holy Spirit.

One of the greatest prayers or treatments ever written is included among the writings of Isaiah, and is known to us as Chapter 35. This chapter number, as we have seen, is purely an arbitrary designation. The chapter itself has nothing in particular to do with either Chapter 34 or Chapter 36. That number has no more intrinsic significance than the number a book may bear on a shelf of a library. As this chapter constitutes a particularly beautiful and effective treatment for any purpose, we shall now consider it at length.

The first thing we notice is that in its literary form it is a glorious poetic rhapsody. The writer, in contemplating the wonder and the love of God, rises to a white heat of spiritual exaltation. The leaden shoes of fear and doubt that glue us to the earth in our everyday lives are cast aside, and he rises on the pinions of Divine Inspiration into the region where all our petty limitations and handicaps vanish in the splendor of the Divine Presence. For the time being he leaves behind him every small and mean thing that keeps a man from God, from joy and freedom. And as he has succeeded in enshrining this transcendent experience in words that still live and glow today with much of his own original divine ecstasy, it becomes possible for us in using this prayer with spiritual understanding, to kindle our own torch from the same fire, and, if we can tune ourselves in with his note, to transcend also any particular difficulty or group of difficulties that may be oppressing us.

The wilderness and the solitary place shall be glad for them; and the desert shall rejoice, and blossom as the rose. The first thing that strikes us here is that the writer is, of course, as all Biblical writers are, an Oriental, and therefore he will give his message in the language and idiom of the orient. This is so obvious that one would think it unnecessary to mention it did we not know how many European and American people down to the last generation were in the habit of taking every oriental simile and flourish at its face value, and often trying to apply it with the utmost literalness to some condition of life in London, or Manchester, or Chicago.

He begins his prayer in the best possible way that a prayer can begin, by a splendid act of faith in God. Always begin your prayers with an act of faith. Remember that Jesus tells us that faith in the Love of God will literally move mountains. And so our Oriental Prophet starts with what is doubtless the greatest affirmation of faith in God of which an Oriental is capable. He looks to God and cries: *The wilderness and the solitary place shall be glad...and the desert shall rejoice and blossom as the rose.* Think of it; the oriental desert to become a garden, to blossom as a rose, to be a center of prosperity and riches. Nothing in our human experience can seem on the face of it less probable than this. No human trouble could be more difficult than this problem of turning the desert into a smiling garden. But with God all things are possible, absolutely all things, anything; and so to Him the redemption of a desert wilderness is just as easy as anything else.

The Bible is predominantly the book of a desert people. Always as the great drama of the Bible story moves across the stage of time, we are conscious of the desert as the background against which it moves. Palestine, a narrow strip of land not much bigger than Wales, was hemmed in by a desert on three sides, and by the unfamiliar and to them unattractive sea on the fourth. Almost everything that came into Palestine came across a desert. Goods and merchandise made their slow way in the leisurely desert caravans. All visitors who came to that country came through the desert and arrived wearied and parched with its sand and dust; and any new ideas that might filter into the world of Palestine had to filter through the desert too, and would inevitably arrive, like the travelers themselves, bearing about them something of the same desert atmosphere. For, just as to people living in the British Isles the sea is always the background — it is the sea that has molded their history, and conditions their everyday lives, even though they may live so far from the ocean that they have never seen it — so the people of Palestine though they might never venture into the wilderness itself, were shaped and governed from first to last by the eternal, unchanging desert, and the conditions of life that spring from a desert home. Always the desert haunted them. There is not a page in the Bible in which we do not vaguely sense the eternal sands and hear the distant tinkle of the camel bells.

And so for us of the West it calls for a distinct effort of the imagination truly to appreciate this splendid declaration with which the poet opens his prayer. He takes the one condition above all others with which man had been totally unable to deal, much less to conquer -- the desert; the one condition perhaps which would seem to him as an Oriental to be eternal and unchangeable, the one condition, we may say, that it would be utterly hopeless to think of changing; and he declares that the goodness and love of God shall completely conquer this. How complete and thorough that conquest is to be is signified by piling up, in the Eastern way, symbol upon symbol — *it shall rejoice and blossom as the rose* — one of the richest and most splendid of God's creations, calling for a special quality of soil and particular care in its culture.

It shall blossom abundantly, and rejoice even with joy and singing; the glory of Lebanon shall be given unto it, the excellency of Carmel and Sharon, they shall see the glory of the Lord and the excellency of our God. On and on he goes in pursuit of his great theme. The glory of the desert redeemed is to be in proportion to its former barrenness. It shall rejoice with joy and singing. Glory of every kind shall be heaped upon it, the especial glory that the Poet knew in his time as only to be found among the cedars of Lebanon; the austere grandeur that he felt only in Carmel; and the sweet, fragrant peace that he had known among the beautifully kept gardens of Sharon. He closes this first stanza, his opening declaration of faith, by reaffirming *They shall see the glory of the Lord, and the excellency of our God.*

In reading this carefully we begin to catch something of the Prophet's own divine faith in the goodness of God, and as faith is infectious, we find the power of his understanding gradually fanning our tiny spark of it into a flame.

Below each level of thought in the Bible there always lies yet a deeper level for those who can find it, and so it is here. Lebanon, Carmel, and Sharon in detail stand for certain spiritual faculties in the soul of man that gradually develop as he persists along the pathway of spiritual awakening, and the Prophet here implies, for those who can understand, that these definite spiritual gifts are the outcome of such prayers as this. Of course, the desert or wilderness is a general term for any kind of trouble or difficulty. It may be a specific problem that you have to overcome, or, in the wider sense, the general state of feeling cut off from God, of which we are all

so conscious to our sorrow.

It is interesting to note that, in a very wonderful and different sense, the desert may be taken to symbolize that state of mind in which man has attained to a high degree of concentration upon God. Sooner or later you will have to put God first in your life, that is to say, your own true spiritual development must become the only thing that really matters. It need not, perhaps had better not be, the only thing in your life, but it must be the first thing. When this happens you will find that you have got rid of a great deal of the unnecessary junk that most people carry about; mental junk, of course, although physical junk is very apt to follow upon this. You will find that you will do a great deal less running about after things that do not matter and only waste your time and energy, when once you have put God first. Your life will become simpler and quieter, but in the true sense, richer and infinitely more worth while.

This has usually happened in the desert. The true desert wanderer has few physical possessions, none of our artificial needs, and few of our so-called comforts; yet he is among the happiest of the human race. Commonly he fears nothing in life or in death. It was an Arab sitting at the door of his tent at night, free from the burden of useless possessions, his mind and heart clarified by simple living, who gazed up at the myriad golden stars so bright in the eastern sky; looked about him with uninterrupted gaze to the distant dusky horizon; and said, "The desert is the garden of Allah."

Strengthen ye the weak hands, and confirm the feeble knees. Say to them that are of a fearful heart, Be strong, fear not; behold, your God will come with vengeance, even God with a recompense; he will come and save you. The first stanza of this wonderful poem-prayer having led the reader to make a splendid declaration of faith, this, the second stanza, takes up definitely the task of working upon his consciousness direct. It says *strengthen ye the weak hands.* Here we meet one of the most important symbols to be found in the Bible — the hand. The hand, briefly, stands for the power of manifestation, or the capacity to express God's ideas on the physical plane. It is the power of getting things done. It is the power of making demonstrations, as we say, or of getting answers to prayer, and so the expression, *strengthen ye the weak hands,* is a command that we are to rise up out of limitation, refuse to put up with it, and insist upon harmony and freedom; that, in fact, we ought always to pray and not to faint. Jesus has told us by means of two separate parables that we are not to accept less than harmony; that we are to go on praying until we make our demonstration; that we are not to take "no" for an answer. And here the inspired writer teaches the same lesson. You should never "put up" with anything. You should never be content to accept less than harmony, peace, and freedom. Until you get these things you must be insistent in prayer.

This particular symbol is a very interesting one. Man is, in his true nature, a spiritual being, a spark from the Divine Fire, but this divine spark, the I Am, has to be embodied, and the human body with which we are familiar, which we all carry about with us, is really but an embodiment of the various faculties and capacities of the Divine I Am. Actually we are at present seeing this embodiment in a very, very limited way, even in the case of the most healthy and beautiful bodies; nevertheless that is what it is. The real self, or I Am, has the power of manifesting absolutely any idea or set of ideas which he can understand, even to some extent; and this power we see embodied as the hand. In all ages the hand has been understood symbolically in this way. We speak of a thing being handy. A person who performs all sorts of essential business for another is often spoken of as his "right hand." At banquets the guest of honor is placed at the right hand of the host. The Christ Truth "sitteth at the right hand of God, the Father Almighty" -- it is the Christ nature that manifests God through man. The word for hand, in Latin, is *manus* and this is derived originally from a Sanskrit word meaning the thinker. Our English word "man" ultimately derives from the same root and carries the same implicit meaning. And we know that it is man's *raison d'etre* to manifest God. Man the manifestor is or should be the hand of God through which God works, and this he is through his power of thought, because he is essentially a thinker. When we wish to paralyze a man's activities we handcuff him, thereby putting his hands out of action, and to have both hands amputated is reckoned as almost complete disablement.

Confirm the feeble knees. This is a very obvious figure for getting rid of fear. There are not many of the sons of men who have not at some time or other known what it was to feel their knees almost literally going from under them through nervousness or fear. Such a condition, unless overcome, is the prelude to the total collapse of the body in what we call a faint. Now when people are in grave difficulties and are beginning to lose their courage — and to lose courage is to lose all — the soul may very aptly be described as being in this condition. The Prophet therefore strikes boldly at our weak hands and feeble knees and proceeds to confirm them, or make them firm, by bringing to mind the truth about God. One might well say indeed that essentially scientific prayer or treatment is just this thing of pausing to *recollect the truth about God.* We do not try to do something with our prayers in the sense of seeking to manipulate things to our liking. Such a proceeding would be will power and not prayer, but we pause in the current of material things and *recollect* what we know to be the truth about God. This acceptation and reaffirmation of the Truth is what brings a spiritual demonstration.

The Prophet says with unanswerable simplicity: *Behold your God will come with vengeance, even God with a recompense. He will come and save you.* And why? Because you are saying your prayers. Because, instead of being carried away in the tide of difficulty as the "heathen" or non-pray-er is, you have paused to recollect the truth about God. You have made the magnificent declaration of faith in the first stanza, and so the action of God will now come into your life with vengeance or vindication.

People sometimes wonder why a loving God should allow them to get into trouble at all in the first place, or why He does not help them without waiting for their prayers. The answer is that we have free will. This is the most precious of all things for us because it is our identity in God as the I Am. If God were to interfere in our lives without our having called upon Him through prayer, our free will would be abrogated, and we should lose our identity. Actually this could not happen, because it would be against the Law of Being. We have to know here that this word "vengeance" in the Bible is a technical term meaning *vindication.* Needless to say, God, Infinite Mind, is not capable of approaching anything like what is known among men as revenge. What happens is that the action of God following upon your prayer *vindicates* the Law of Being, and as this Law is the law of perfect good you are saved. The demonstration may figuratively be described as the recompense for your treatment.

Then the eyes of the blind shall be opened, and the ears of the deaf shall be unstopped. Then shall the lame man leap as an hart, and the tongue of the dumb sing; for in the wilderness shall waters break out, and streams in the desert. These two phrases constitute one of the most wonderful passages in the whole Bible. There is no other that can quite be put beside it. It is a song of triumph, and joy, and liberation, probably the most glorious celebration of the power of God in prayer that ever was written. Think what it promises, what it announces to be the natural result of spiritual prayer.

— The eyes of the blind shall be opened, and the ears of the deaf shall be unstopped, the lame man shall leap as an hart, and the tongue of the dumb shall sing! Is this a sufficient manifesto of spiritual healing? Is anything of importance left out? Can we, in the face of this, declare that any physical condition is beyond the reach of prayer? Can we dare say or think any more that with God some things are possible, and some things are not? The blind, the deaf, the dumb, and the crippled are to be set free and restored to health by the power of God.

Spiritual healing is one of the most glorious manifestations of the Universal Christ. It is the Beautiful Gate of the Temple, but it is not everything. It is the spiritual gift that has been most emphasized in the metaphysical movement for two or three generations, but as Paul was careful to imply in his enumeration, it is only one gift. The healing of the body is essential, but the thing that really matters of course is the spiritual development of the soul. What is a physical healing but the outer evidence that a step in spiritual development has been taken; and the physical healings enumerated here fully and beautifully as they apply to the physical body, are still more important when raised to a higher level.

It is glorious that the physical eyes of the physically blind should be opened, but the physical eyes symbolize man's power of spiritual perception; and the magnificent promise of these two verses particularly implies that the gift of spiritual perception is to be acquired by prayer; and that when we earnestly pray for it nothing can prevent our getting it.

It is glorious that the ears of the physically deaf should be unstopped; but hearing, on the higher level, stands for spiritual understanding, and it is ten times more important that spiritually obtuse people obtain an understanding of the truth about God and about life.

It is glorious that the physically crippled should regain his strength so that, throwing away his crutches and straightening his back, he shall assume the birthright of healthy manhood and run and leap like a deer. But it is ten times more important that moral and spiritual cripples should succeed in surmounting their infirmities and rise up in the free exercise of spiritual faculty and prayer.

It is glorious that the physically dumb should acquire the power of the physical word to speak and sing; but the tongue stands also for man's spiritual dominion or power, and it is a thousand times more important for the spiritually dumb, those men and women who have no power of spiritual demonstration, to acquire the power of the Logos or Creative Word which is their divine inheritance, and learn to use it with telling effect for themselves and others.

Never before or since has the importance of these things both physical and spiritual been brought home so convincingly to men's hearts as here. And by way of a final emphasis on these transcendent truths the Oriental Prophet repeats his supreme argument: *For in the wilderness shall waters break out, and streams in the desert. And the parched ground shall become a pool, and the thirsty land springs of water.* To the oriental reader no claim for Divine Power could seem to out-reach this.

As we have seen, the sandy desert is to him the one eternal and unchanging fact, and to say that it shall be plenteously filled with water is to include all promises. We need to remember that, in that eastern land, water is considered the most precious of all substances; comparatively small quantities are often transported miles upon miles upon the backs of camels and mules, and in remote desert places a cup of water is literally worth its weight in gold — far more perhaps, for it may mean the difference between life and death. We in the West who seldom know a real shortage of water, whose climate is, if anything, a trifle too wet for comfort, have to use our imagination again in order that we may realize how powerful and telling this simile really is, and all that it conveys of the power, and majesty, and resources, and love of God.

In the habitation of dragons, where each lay, shall be grass with reeds and rushes. As the result of prayer, of the recollection of the Omnipresence of God, and the affirmation of faith in His goodness, we are to lose our fear; regain our power of manifesting harmony and peace; obtain our physical healing, no matter what the malady may have been; and above all, we are to develop spiritual perception, spiritual understanding, the power of speaking the Word with effect, and to acquire the capacity to develop new spiritual faculties altogether, for which there are no words in ordinary language. (We are but lame men without these faculties.) And now the Prophet says significantly: *In the habitation of dragons where each lay, shall be grass with reeds and rushes.* This is a very remarkable and significant statement. The writer of this wonderful treatment knew all there is to be known about human nature. Our psychological experts are just beginning to scratch the surface of this subject; nevertheless much good work has been done by what is called the new psychology, in spite of its manifest errors; and people are just beginning to realize the existence of those "dark unfathomed caves" of our nature that are nowadays called the subconscious mind. We are beginning to realize that a thought is not dead or powerless merely because we are not consciously thinking it; but that it has simply floated out of sight under the ice, as it were, carrying with it all the potentialities that it had for evil, and much more in addition, now that it is out of sight. We are beginning to understand that a thing is not destroyed because it is suppressed, but, on the contrary, just as compression increases tremendously the detonating power of an explosive, so thoughts and feelings, and especially feelings that for one reason or another we do not care to face frankly, acquire an incalculable access of power for evil when they are suppressed into the subconscious and become what we call complexes. Indeed, psychotherapeutics has proved that a very large share of all our temporal ills spring from these very things. Now, Isaiah knew all this, and his name for these complexes is *dragons,* and a very good name too. It would be difficult to find a better one. And here he promises that as a result of prayer the dragons shall be cleared out and destroyed, and the watery depths where each lay shall become a secure and peaceful mead — quiet with grass and reeds and rushes.

And an highway shall be there, and a way, and it shall be called The way of holiness. We now come to one of the transcendent revelations of the Bible. For sheer power and splendor this passage stands alone. The whole stanza is quite unmatched either in scripture or elsewhere. The Prophet rises higher and higher on the inspirational tide that bears him onward as he envisions the complete salvation of mankind that shall be. His eye sweeps along the whole flood of spiritual evolution, right on to the uttermost bounds where the human and the Divine shall be merged in final Unity.

For the individual, too, it is the promise and the means for the triumphant journey back to God. It is the great manifesto of salvation, the complete statement of the way of escape from limitation, sin, sickness, and death.

And an highway shall be there, and a way, and it shall be called The way of holiness. This is a definite and, one may say, businesslike statement that there is to be a way out. It means that it is no longer to be necessary for man to put up with anything less than perfect harmony. It really means that resignation to anything less than peace, health, and harmony — so far from being a virtue — will become what it has actually become, a breach of the Law of Being. Let us make no mistake about this. Now that this way has been opened, resignation to limitation and inharmony is nothing but a fine name for laziness and cowardice. The Prophet definitely says that there shall be a highway. Now what is a highway? Is it not a public main road, accessible to everybody, which all those who observe the law use with equal right? No one has any authority to put a barrier on the highway, to fence it off to the exclusion of certain people, or to exercise any kind of proprietary rights whatever. That is what a highway is, and the Prophet here definitely says that the Path of freedom and salvation is to be a highway. No man, no organization, no rules and regulations of either the dead or the living, have any power or authority whatever to forbid anyone to that highway, or to make any terms upon which he shall enter it. No conditions of membership, no entrance fees or entrance ceremonials have any authority from the inspired word. It is public. It is open. It is free.

Having prophesied a highway, the writer then definitely states that it will be a Way. Now a "way," of course, is a technical term meaning a way back to the consciousness of the Real Presence of God. It is what we often call The Path. And we may pause for a moment here to realize the tremendous importance of the statement that the Path is a *highway*. Most religious movements, at any rate the older and greater ones, have taught of the Path and how to enter upon it. But always they had treated it, not as a highway, but as a private road fenced in by themselves, to the gates of which they alone held the keys. The Bible, however, came to the world to break down this exclusiveness and to say that the Way is a highway. It is really impossible for the student to over-stress the importance of this fact. Again and again and again throughout history the open highway has been given to the people for a short time, only to be closed up again, and before very long, and usually by the very people who had opened it. So grave are the dangers that attend organized religion, so powerful and so subtle are the evils resulting from the accumulation of much property (an evil which overtakes almost every well organized church sooner or later), that unless we keep this point constantly fresh in our minds, we may be in danger of repeating the old mistakes.

The Prophet goes on to say that the Way or the Path is the path of holiness. Now, of course, we need to understand that the Bible uses the word holiness in a very much wider and more far-reaching sense than the usual one. The word "holiness" really means wholeness, not just holiness of character, rare and wonderful as that is, but complete holiness of life. This includes perfect bodily health — no invalid is holy in the Bible sense, however spiritual he may be in other respects — it includes the idea of happiness or true peace of mind, of prosperity, which means freedom from nagging fears concerning the necessities of life; in fact, holiness means all-round health, prosperity, and spiritual harmony. Actually the words whole, holy, wholesome, heal, and healing, all go back to the same old English root, because they are but different aspects of the same thing.

This does not in the least detract from the transcendent importance of what is usually designated holiness, the thing to which a great modern Rationalist referred to sadly when he said "Holiness, deepest of all words that defy definition."

The Prophet goes on to say of this glorious highway, *the unclean shall not pass over it.* Now exactly what does this mean? Too often it has been supposed to imply that the ordinary human being, full of faults and shortcomings, and, still more, one conscious of graver sin, has no chance upon that highway; that it is reserved for the saint and the spiritual hero — for those who are indeed clean. Yet nothing could possibly be farther from the truth. What point could there be in providing a highway for those who are already "saved." Did not our Lord say, "The well need not a physician, but those who are sick." And indeed to suppose otherwise would be like saying that one should not use soap until his hands were clean. The fact is, you do not bring a clean heart to God that He may love you for it; you bring your unclean heart to Him in order that He may cleanse it. The real meaning of this magnificent statement, the real bearing of this whole glorious final stanza, is that the highway shall be provided for the average human being, the "wayfaring man," you and me who stand in need of purification and salvation. The "unclean" are those very thoughts and beliefs of limitation, sin, sickness, fear, doubt, and so forth, that are the only things keeping us out of the Kingdom of Heaven today. These are the unclean; and once we are upon that highway they have no more power to hinder our progress. Their power of keeping us back in the darkness is gone.

No longer need frail, weak human beings fear to approach the highway. *It shall be for those.*

The wayfaring men, though fools, shall not err therein. Having shown that no degree of weakness or guilt can keep a man off the Path, if he really wants to enter upon it, Isaiah here takes up the other point that no lack of intellectual power or intellectual training can exclude him either. No want of what is called cleverness, or what is generally called education, makes any difference here. The most brilliant academic career, and the simplest unlettered background, are equally unimportant, provided there is the right intention, reinforced by right application. As a matter of fact, intellectual brilliance and much secular knowledge have kept many people off of this Path because, under our modern system of education, these things are very apt to beget spiritual pride. On the other hand, a good sound intelligence, while not in the least a guarantee of spiritual power, is likely to be very helpful in spiritual development, because it enables the candidate to appreciate the need for thoroughness, faithfulness, and disinterestedness; and it leads him to check up his results in order to insure that he really is making progress as time goes on. It saves him from living in a fool's paradise by supposing that he is demonstrating when he is not. It enables him to distinguish between spiritual progress and mere emotional indulgence. The great point is that we do not have to bring knowledge or wisdom to the Path, but that it is the function of the Path to equip us with these things.

No lion shall be there, nor any ravenous beast shall go up thereon, it shall not be found there; but the redeemed shall walk there. Here the whole story is repeated in another form, in accordance with the Eastern poetical tradition, which drives home its points by means of variety of iteration. Once upon the Path, troubles and difficulties will indeed still come to us, for a time at least; but now they come up from the inside, so to say; they emerge from the depths of our own personality, because they have no business to be there, and are to be dealt with once and for all. No longer are they lions or ravenous beasts from which we need to be protected; but rather are they problems to be solved once and for all, that we may be free forever.

And now this wonderful poem finishes up with one of the supreme verses of the whole Bible. Having entered and walked the Path, learned the lessons, and won the crown of completed understanding, our limitations and our spectral fears — for specters they are, that and nothing more — disappear forever; and the glory of the Union, the grand transformation, is completed. Old things are passed away and *the ransomed of the Lord return, and come to Zion with songs and everlasting joy upon their heads: they shall obtain joy and gladness, and sorrow and sighing shall flee away.* Did ever man write like this? The "ransomed of the Lord" are of course those who have realized, not merely believed, but realized their oneness with their own Indwelling Christ; realized that that Indwelling Christ is in reality and truth themselves, not near to, not belonging to, but identical with themselves. Such are they who really have demonstrated the I Am.

And they shall return and come to Zion. Zion is the direct realization of God. Jerusalem is the highest thing in the human consciousness less than the Divine contact, but Zion is the realization of God Himself. It is to this that the Souls Triumphant will come, and, says the poet, with songs and everlasting joy upon their heads. They are to come singing, he says, and this is significant, for a spontaneous song is our natural expression of the highest joy. The instinct of the human soul which has not been cramped by taboos and inhibitions is to burst into song when it feels happy and free; and so the Bible rightly uses the idea of singing to express utter and spontaneous joy. And note that it says "everlasting" joy, no joy that may fade away with the lapse of time or the coming of some unexpected cloud. This joy is to be the joy of God, that never can and never will wane when once we have found it. So precise and thorough is the Bible's expounding of the way of man's salvation that here it makes a point of putting the joy upon their heads. Now the human head symbolizes always the Christ understanding of Truth, as distinct from mere blind faith, or simple emotional groping; and so here we see that this divine joy is to be the joy of perfect *understanding,* which is the only real guarantee of permanence.

Our poem terminates its glorious upward sweep with a final clinching assurance, much as one might comfort a doubting child, an assurance that all this is really true, saying in the simplest language: *Sorrow and sighing shall flee away.*

55752637R00017

Made in the USA
San Bernardino, CA
05 November 2017